Did you know

Whistler's mo

J. Paul Getty had a pay telephone installed in his English country house so he couldn't be charged with his guests' calls?

Hans Christian Andersen was so afraid of being buried alive that he habitually left a note beside his bed: "I only *seem* dead"?

Sensitive little Leo Tolstoy's brothers called him "Lyova Ryova"—Russian for "Leo Cry Baby"?

Pablo Picasso couldn't learn the letters of the alphabet?

NOT A GOOD WORD ABOUT ANYBODY is ...

NOT A
GOOD WORD
ABOUT
ANYBODY

Jane Goodsell

BALLANTINE BOOKS • NEW YORK

Grateful acknowledgment is made to the following for permission to reprint previously published material:

Alfred A. Knopf, Inc.: excerpt from HEARTBURN by Nora Ephron. Copyright © 1983 by Nora Ephron. Reprinted by permission of Alfred A. Knopf, Inc.

Doubleday & Company, Inc.: excerpt from the poem ''Mehitabel and Her Kittens'' by Don Marquis; excerpt from ''The Recessional'' by Rudyard Kipling from *The Collected Verse of Rudyard Kipling.* Reprinted by permission of Doubleday & Company, Inc.

Frank Music Corp.: excerpt from the lyrics to ''Luck be a Lady'' by Frank Loesser from ''Guys and Dolls.'' Copyright 1950 by Frank Music Corp. Copyright renewed 1978 by Frank Music Corp. International copyright secured. All rights reserved. Used by permission.

Grove Press, Inc.: excerpt from TROPIC OF CAPRICORN by Henry Miller. Copyright © 1961 by Grove Press, Inc. Reprinted by arrangement with Grove Press, Inc.

Harper & Row Publisher, Inc.: quote from CHARLOTTE'S WEB by E.B. White. Copyright 1952 by E.B. White. Text copyright renewed 1980 by E.B. White. Reprinted by permission of Harper & Row Publisher, Inc.

Herald Square Music, Inc.: excerpt from the lyrics to ''The Little Things You do Together'' by Stephen Sondheim. Copyright © 1970 by Range Road Music, Inc., Quartet Music, Inc. and Rilting Music, Inc. Used by permission. All rights reserved.

Little, Brown and Company and Curtis Brown Ltd.: excerpt from the poem ''Family Court'' from VERSES FROM 1929 ON by Ogden Nash. Copyright 1931 by Ogden Nash. (Renewed.) First appeared in *The Saturday Evening Post.* Also published in PARENTS KEEP OUT by Ogden Nash; excerpt from the poem ''You and Me and P.B. Shelley'' from VERSES FROM 1929 ON by Ogden Nash. Copyright 1942 by Ogden Nash. (Renewed.) First appeared in *The Saturday Evening Post.* Also published in PARENTS KEEP OUT by Ogden Nash. Reprinted by permission of Little, Brown and Company and Curtis Brown Ltd.

McGraw-Hill Publishers: excerpts from THE NAKED APE by Desmond Morris. Copyright © 1967 by Desmond Morris. Reprinted by permission of McGraw-Hill Publishers.

Oxford University Press: excerpt from ''George the Third'' from THE COMPLETE CLERIHEWS of E. Clerihew Bentley, 1981. Reprinted by permission of Oxford University Press.

Library of Congress Catalog Card Number: 87-91387

ISBN 0-345-34036-1

Manufactured in the United States of America

First Edition: March 1988

Dedicated, with love and thanks,
to my daughter Ann

. . . If you come to think of it, what a queer thing Life is!
So unlike anything else, don't you know, if you see what I mean.

—P. G. Wodehouse

Contents

Foreword

Were it not for the misfortunes of our friends, life would be unbearable.

—François, Duc de La Rochefoucauld (1613–1680)

This book is a collection of the misfortunes of others. La Rochefoucauld to the contrary, not a one is likely to be a friend of yours. Some you wouldn't touch with a ten-foot pole, much less invite to dinner. Even so, their problems and predicaments may help you to view your own more philosophically.

In this crisis-fraught world it is essential to know how to calm yourself down and cheer yourself up when things go wrong. One way is to chuck the whole sorry mess and run off to Tahiti. A more mature approach is to develop perspective, to become aware you're not the only person in this world who's got problems. You already know that, of course. You listen to the news, you read "Dear Abby," you watch *Dynasty*. You're not so self-centered as to think you alone are plagued by blighted dreams and a sense of your inadequacies. Everybody's got troubles, right?

Well, sure. But it has been my own experience that the more I need to be reassured on that score, the more life conspires to convince me otherwise. When a romance wanes or a financial venture collapses, I am bombarded with news of other people's rapturous liaisons and financial triumphs. If I drag myself to a party in the hope it will lift my spirits, everyone I talk to is doing *Great! Fabulous! Terrific!* I am surrounded by high-achievers enthusing about the slalom course at Gstaad and comparing high tech accessories on their Alfa Romeos. Or else they've just endowed a chair of philosophy or been honored with a civic award.

I do occasionally encounter persons willing, even eager, to confess to problems. But not to problems they've got. These are problems they once had, but conquered. Slimmed down from a size 20½ to a size 8. Or pulled out of Chapter 11 bankruptcy to find a more meaningful existence and a steady six-figure income in a tofu franchise.

If you don't get what I'm talking about, you must be a wonderful, compassionate human being whose heart fills with joy, rather than envy, at the good fortune of others. Either that or you've got more trophies and a better Alfa Romeo than anyone else.

But if you now and then wish you could think of someone (besides Job) who's as hapless as you, take heart. You now have an alternative to Valium and melancholy. This book.

—Jane Goodsell

Acknowledgments

My gratitude to Professor of Biology Laurens Ruben, who patiently answered my many questions; to Professor of Botany John A. West for his expertise on chocolate; to Jack Radow, who kept me supplied with books; to Aphra Katzev for gifts of time; to Ruth Manary for being the best of friends.

Nobody's Perfect

Aristotle bit his fingernails.

President Ulysses S. Grant was arrested and fined twenty dollars for exceeding the Washington D.C. speed limit on his horse.

Charles I pawned the crown jewels of England.

Whistler's mother opened other people's mail.

J. Paul Getty had a pay telephone installed in his English country house so he couldn't be charged for his guests' calls.

Composer Jacques Offenbach was one of the most elegantly dressed men in nineteenth century Paris, except when he didn't remember—as he often didn't—to button his fly.

Playwright George S. Kaufman ate almost nothing but chocolate.

Louis XVI and J. Edgar Hoover were both terrified of black cats.

Napoleon, Karl Marx, and Marilyn Monroe suffered from hemorrhoids.

Horatio Alger wrote over one hundred moralistic books about boys who worked hard, saved their pennies, led virtuous lives, and were rewarded with fame and fortune. Alger's own life was not so exemplary. When in his thirties and a Unitarian minister, he was dismissed from his pulpit on a morals charge involving young boys. He also failed to follow his own financial admonitions. Horatio Alger died a poor man.

President Kennedy confided to John Kenneth Galbraith that one of the unexpected pleasures of his job was reading FBI reports on the scandalous doings of his appointees. Even the most decorous had some eyebrow-raisers in their files.

In her 1981 autobiography, *Nancy*, Mrs. Reagan post-dated her birth, subtracting two years from her age.

Alfred Hitchcock's idea of a terrific joke was to ply a cameraman with brandy laced with a potent laxative, then dare him to spend the night in a deserted studio chained to a camera.

Dr. Samuel Johnson was a skip-around who never read a book straight through.

President McKinley bit his cigars in two and chewed on them.

Novelist John P. Marquand was a rich penny-pincher who made a terrible scene over an airmail stamp, to him an outrageous extravagance.

Pope Alexander VI won his election in 1492 by bribery.

Harry Houdini, the great magician and escape artist, was a compulsive personality who couldn't spend an unproductive moment. At parties, Houdini would take off his shoes and socks so he could practise tying knots with a piece of string threaded around his toes.

To enhance his ascetic image, Lord Byron ate only crackers and soda water in public. In private, when he thought nobody was looking, he wolfed down meat and potatoes.

Thomas Jefferson wrote a friend that the world would be far better off without dogs.

Playwright Richard Sheridan totally ignored his mail.

According to a survey, fifteen percent of Americans bite their toenails.

The Duke of Windsor saw no reason why he should ever pick up a check.

It's not surprising that George Washington usually wrote his wife's letters for her. Martha's mystifying spelling and grammar are evident in a letter she wrote to a London merchant:

> *I have sent a night gound to be dide of an fashonob corler fitt for me to ware and beg you would have it dide better that I sent las year that was very badly don this gound is of a good lenght for me.*

Sigmund Freud never traveled alone because he didn't know how to read a railroad timetable.

Film director King Vidor was a pack rat who couldn't even throw out a laundry receipt.

Prime Minister Clement Atlee didn't always find time in the morning to read the London *Times* but he never missed working the crossword puzzle.

It's impossible to be more flat-chested than I am.

—Candice Bergen

Four Fifth Avenue jewelers, including Van Cleef & Arpels and Tiffany, pleaded guilty to helping their customers evade sales taxes. Company records were falsified to indicate that purchases were sent to out-of-state addresses, in which case they would not have been subject to sales taxes. Actually only empty boxes were sent, and the customers left the stores with their purchases (average price, forty thousand dollars) in their hands.

W.C. Fields so distrusted banks that he divided his money among several hundred of them all over the world.

The owner of Aurora, an elegant Manhattan restaurant, admits to a not-so-elegant passion for store-bought cookies, particularly "the one with the coconut-sprinkled pink-marshmallow topping."

Journalist John Gunther found Albert Schweitzer "dictatorial, irascible, and somewhat vain."

There's a good deal of human nature in man.

—Artemus Ward

More than a million Britishers told an opinion poll they would not have moved to their present homes if they had known what irritating neighbors they'd have. Those in town mostly grumbled that the people next door were "too nosy" and "too noisy" or had annoying pets. In the country, complaints focused on fences and drains.

President Taft often dozed off during cabinet meetings.

Lillian Hellman so lacked a sense of direction she got lost on her own property.

George Washington turned down the $500-a-month salary offered him as commander-in-chief of the Continental Army, insisting he had no desire to profit from the war and wanted only to be reimbursed for his expenses. At war's end, he submitted a bill for $414,108.21 plus $7,488 in interest and $27,665.30 for his wife's expenses when she visited him at Valley Forge. His bill covered wines (excellent French vintages), his eight personal servants, and his clothes (velvet coats and Belgian-lace ruffles.) When he was elected president, he again offered to work for expenses only, but Congress insisted on paying him $25,000 a year. Marvin Kitman, author of *George Washington's Expense Account*, called this decision "the country's first economy drive."

Queen Victoria kept her palace so cold, and the conversation at her table so stilted, that an invitation to dine with her was cause for lamentation.

John Masefield, author of "Sea-Fever" ("I must down to the sea again . . ."), and Admiral Horatio Nelson both suffered from seasickness.

General de Gaulle permitted no one to speak to him when he played solitaire. His sense of manifest destiny made it essential that he win, but his dignity precluded cheating. His solution was to change the rules of the game to make winning easier.

Hans Christian Andersen was so afraid of being buried alive that he habitually left beside his bed a note: "I only *seem* dead."

Cardinal Wolsey, whose lofty arrogance only Henry VIII dared to defy, compelled bishops to tie his shoelaces and made servants attend him on their knees.

New Yorker editor Harold Ross called James Thurber "the greatest unlistener I know."

King George II had temper tantrums in which he kicked his wig all over the room.

A survey of U.S. corporations revealed that executives waste an average of four weeks a year looking for things they can't find or waiting for their secretaries to find them.

Honoré de Balzac picked his nose in public.

Forty per cent of the participants in a 1986 *People* magazine poll admitted they would not report a bank error made in their favor by a machine.

In one of his habitual states of absentmindedness, novelist G. K. Chesterton telegraphed his wife: "Am in Market Harborough. Where ought I to be?"

Paul Newman is color-blind. So was Abraham Lincoln.

Mr. and Mrs. Benjamin Harrison were so intimidated by the new-fangled electricity installed in the White House that they didn't dare touch the switches. If there were no servants around to turn off the lights when the Harrisons went to bed, they slept with them on.

According to a 1986 Harris poll, only twenty-one percent of adult Americans are within their recommended weight range, and a mere eight percent exercise rigorously every day.

Karl Marx was turned down for a job with a railroad company because of his atrocious handwriting.

Mamie Eisenhower seldom got up before noon.

Surveys reveal that fifty-five percent of the inhabitants of Iceland believe in elves.

Cary Grant flunked his first screen test because the director thought his neck too thick.

Louis Pasteur had such an irrational fear of dirt and infection that he refused to shake hands.

Walt Disney was prejudiced against Jews, blacks, and labor unions. He didn't think much of women either.

E. B. White was a hypochondriac to whom every sore throat was cancer of the larynx. He once diagnosed as a brain tumor a condition that turned out to be a bad sunburn.

The average American woman is five feet four inches tall, and weighs 142 pounds.

President Kennedy, a cigar smoker himself, slapped a ban on the import of Cuban cigars. But first he dispatched couriers to buy up every good Cuban cigar in the city of Washington.

Tennessee Williams was fired by the Gotham Book Mart because he was so inept at wrapping packages.

Rev. Henry Ward Beecher, the highest paid preacher in the U.S. in the late nineteenth century, accepted one thousand dollars for endorsing a truss.

King Alfonso of Spain was so tone-deaf he couldn't recognize his own country's national anthem.

Man was made at the end of the week, when God was tired.

—Mark Twain

Other Children's Parents

Parenthood can be very demoralizing. Unless you can stay on your best behavior during the twenty or so years it takes to raise your family, and never lose your patience, never break a promise, and (despite lack of sleep, impossible demands, and constant interruptions) never commit a single one of the grievous wrongs perpetrated against you by your own parents, you're sure to suffer I'm-not-fit-to-raise-a-child guilt pangs.

As an antidote for these mostly undeserved feelings of parental remorse, here's a roundup of mothers and fathers whose mistakes and misdeeds should reassure you that you're not doing the world's worst job of raising kids.

Honoré de Balzac was sent away at the age of seven to a strict boarding school where he had no pocket money and no holidays. In six years his mother visited him twice.

Anthony Trollope's father routed his small son out of bed at six in the morning to recite the Greek alphabet and the rules of Latin grammar. If Anthony made no mistakes, he was rewarded by not getting his hair pulled.

Simone de Beauvoir's father responded to her letters by mailing them back with her mistakes in grammar and spelling corrected.

Thomas Edison's father invited everyone in town to come watch him whip his son in the town square.

In Aaron Burr's letters to his daughter and grandson, he wrote of his sexual encounters with prostitutes, including such details as the price he paid and the degree of his enjoyment.

Leonard Bernstein's mother's cooking was described with no nostalgia by Lenny's younger brother Burton in his book *Family Matters*:

> . . . *she had an utter inability to cook, which flew in the face of the Jewish mother stereotype . . . she would begin the roasting or broiling of meat for dinner as soon as the breakfast dishes were put away. Throughout the day the food was*

placed in the refrigerator for safekeeping and then triumphantly reheated a couple of hours before we seated ourselves at table. . . .

Lord Byron, who was born with a club foot, was called by his mother "a limping brat."

Franklin Roosevelt claimed he never in his life went outdoors without his mother calling after him, "Franklin! Are you sure you're dressed warmly enough?"

The polite and delicate little boy who became Frederick the Great was beaten by his father for falling off a rearing horse and for wearing gloves in cold weather. When Frederick tried to run away, he was put in solitary confinement.

He (my father) *really believed in discipline. So did my mother. Till I was thirteen, I thought my name was "Shut Up."*

—Joe Namath

Most snake mothers are indifferent to their offspring, and snake fathers ignore them completely. Pythons are an exception. They make devoted parents, protective of eggs and children.

Charlemagne was so attached to his daughters that he refused to allow them to marry and leave home. He had no objection to sex, however, and delighted in his many grandchildren.

John Wesley was absolutely forbidden to eat between meals.

The mother of Louis XIV personally selected the courtesan to conduct his sexual initiation.

Mark Twain was invited to lecture at Bryn Mawr when his daughter Susy was a student there. Susy begged her father to please, *please* not tell his favorite ghost story, "The Golden Arm," because she thought it too unsophisticated for Ivy League tastes. Twain promised he wouldn't but told it anyway. A short time later Susy left Bryn Mawr.

I have numerous children whom I see once a day for ten, I hope, awe-inspiring moments.

—Evelyn Waugh

The mother of poet Edwin Arlington Robinson was so disappointed he wasn't a girl that she didn't name him for six months.

Eugene O'Neill became totally estranged from his eldest son and had nothing to do with his daughter, Oona, after she married Charlie Chaplin.

John Ruskin's mother allowed him no friends and no sweets. His only toy was a bunch of keys.

I couldn't even contemplate drinking a glass of milk with my salami sandwich without giving serious offense to God Almighty. Imagine then what my conscience gave me for all that jerking off! The guilt, the fears, the terror bred into my bones! What in their world was not charged wih danger, dripping with germs, fraught with peril? Who filled these parents of mine with such a fearful sense of life . . . ?

Portnoy's Complaint
—Philip Roth

Portnoy's mother's complaint: *Alex, to pick up a phone is such a simple thing—how much longer will I be around to bother you anyway?*

—Philip Roth

The warm and wonderful qualities of Marmee, the archetypical supermom of *Little Women*, were pointedly lacking in Louisa May Alcott's real mother. Abigail Alcott was a sour-tempered and demanding woman who tied six-year-old Louisa to the sofa as punishment for running away, and left notes on her daughter's pillow exhorting her to be a better girl.

President and Mrs. Reagan did not attend the wedding ceremony of Doria Palmieri and their son Ron. And President Reagan did not meet his granddaughter (his and Jane Wyman's adopted son Michael's daughter) until she was almost two years old.

Anne Boleyn was tried for adultery with five men including her own brother. The Earl of Wiltshire made her beheading a certainty by declaring himself convinced of her guilt. He was her father.

Liv Ulmann: . . . *my mother, just the thought of discussing sex with her—though now I think it's easier—but only a few years ago we always pretended like none of us did it, you know. . . .*

When Joseph Conrad's son Borys was born, Conrad wrote to a friend, "My wife will want to show you the blessed baby. I hate babies."

Eleanor Roosevelt's mother called her "Granny" and repeatedly told her she was the ugly ducking in a family of beautiful women.

When Douglas MacArthur left home to attend West Point, his mother went along to make sure her son moved steadily toward his heroic destiny. To keep an eye on him, Mrs. MacArthur found herself an apartment with an unobstructed view into Douglas's dormitory room.

Dr. Spock's mea culpa: "When my wife said about our three-year-old boy, 'He's asked for a doll; shall I get one for him?' I asked in alarm, 'What are you trying to do—turn him into a sissy?' "

Leonard Bernstein's father took a dim view of his son's interest in music, and continually pressured Lenny to give it up and go into the family beauty supply business. Years later, when an interviewer accused him of having tried to subvert his famous son's talent, Mr. Bernstein was unabashed. "How was I to know," he snapped, "that he was *Leonard Bernstein*?"

Sir Thomas More displayed his naked sleeping daughters to a prospective suitor to choose which he liked best. After comparing front and back views of the young ladies, the suitor, Sir William Roper, patted his choice on the bottom and proclaimed, "Thou art mine."

In a divorce suit against her fourth husband, a Los Angeles woman told the judge that she used to call her mother every half hour when she went out because "Mother always wanted to know that I was quite all right."

Mary Ball Washington, George's mum, was an aggravating and sharp-tongued nag who complained constantly that her children neglected her. She was particularly annoyed at her firstborn, George, for running off to be commander-in-chief, when it was his duty to stay home and take care of his mother.

King George V was a stern and forbidding father who rarely spoke to his children except to criticize them. His son, the Duke of Windsor, said in his autobiography that nothing in life could ever so intimidate him as the message that his father wished to see him in the library.

When Gandhi decided to give up sex forever at the age of thirty-six, he expected his sons to follow suit, not surprisingly, they disobeyed and were attacked by their father in the press.

A. A. Milne, author of the beloved Winnie-the-Pooh books, was not the merry, whimsical father one would expect. His real-life son, Christopher, described him as buttoned-up and remote: "Some people are good with children," Christopher wrote. "Others are not . . . my father was a creative writer, and it was precisely because he was *not* able to play with his small son . . . that he wrote about him instead."

When other boys his age had short hair and wore shirts and ties, Christopher Milne's mummy kept his hair long and dressed him in girlish smocks. (He looked like the Shepherd drawings for his father's books.) Mrs. Milne also encouraged Christopher to lisp.

Ulysses S. Grant's mother didn't attend his two inaugurations and never once visited him in the White House.

The female cuckoo can't be bothered to sit on her own eggs. She sneaks them into the nests of other birds, substituting her eggs for theirs, which she tosses out. The surrogate mother, tricked into believing the cuckoo eggs her own, conscientiously hatches them.

Little Lord Fauntleroy called his mother "Dearest." If you can't imagine your children ever addressing you so charmingly, don't feel unduly put down. According to Sigmund Freud, "One of the surest premonitions of later nervousness is when a child shows itself insatiable in its demands for parental tenderness."

Even the happiest child has moments when he wishes his parents were dead.

—Allan Fromme, psychologist

Jessica Mitford is a case in point. Her parents were eccentric and self-centered, but not cruel. Even so, Jessica put every shilling she could muster into her Running Away Account and envied Oliver Twist because "he was so lucky to live in a fascinating orphanage."

If you sometimes view with muted enthusiasm the joys of parenthood, it may comfort you to know that your ambivalence was shared by others as disparate as Ralph Waldo Emerson, William James, and mehitabel the cat:

There never was a child so lovely but his mother was glad to get him asleep.

—Ralph Waldo Emerson

Our three young children are all in Switzerland, the older boy in Munich, and my wife and I are like middle-aged omnibus horses let loose in a pasture. The first holiday we have had together for fifteen years; I feel like a barrel without hoops.

—William James

*it is not archy
that i am shy on mother love
god knows i care for
the sweet little things
curse them
but am i never to be allowed
to live my own life. . . .*

mehitabel and her kittens
—Don Marquis

Other Parents' Children

Who'd have guessed that backward little Albert Einstein would ever amount to anything? The poor kid didn't speak a word till he was four years old. And look how well that dim-witted Churchill boy turned out. For a dullard who kept flunking exams he made quite a name for himself.

Problem children aren't necessarily destined for oblivion or the Most Wanted List. Many of history's most illustrious personages were once dolts, misfits, and scapegraces who drove their parents and teachers to despair.

Louis Pasteur stood fifteenth out of twenty-two in his chemistry class.

Six-year-old Thomas Edison deliberately set his father's barn on fire.

Pablo Picasso couldn't learn the letters of the alphabet.

Eugene O'Neill was expelled from Princeton for throwing a beer bottle through the president's window.

Manuel Laureano Rodríguez y Sanchez was a delicate little mama's boy who grew up to become the great bullfighter Manolete.

Gamal Abdel Nasser failed both the second and third grades. When he flunked out of law school he went into the army.

Henri de Toulouse-Lautrec was a spoiled·brat who insisted on getting his own way. On a visit to the cathedral of Saint Cecile he announced, "I want to pee! Right here!" and promptly did so, on the cathedral's mosaic floor.

You can learn many things from children. How much patience you have, for instance.

—Franklin P. Jones

According to his friend, Charles Lanham, Ernest Hemingway always referred to his mother as "that bitch."

Ogden Nash dropped out of Harvard after one year and went to New York to work as a bond salesman. In two years he sold one bond—to his godmother.

Sarah Bernhardt, the queen of the French stage, known as "the divine Sarah," was an exceptionally shy and awkward teenager.

King George VI (then Prince Albert) was sixty-eighth in a class of sixty-eight at the Royal Naval College.

Enrico Fermi, who grew up to become a noted physicist, was the ringleader of a stink-bomb attack on the faculty of his high school in Pisa.

The Duchess of Orleans, Louis XIV's sister-in-law, immortalized in a letter the creative mischief of a seventeenth century troublemaker. A student at a Jesuit school, the boy persuaded a local artist to paint a pair of saints on his buttocks—Saint Ignatius on the right side, Saint Francis Xavier on the left. Back at school, he misbehaved in his customary fashion until one of the fathers wearily proclaimed his intention to beat him. The boy fell to his knees and cried out, "O Saint Ignatius, O Saint Xavier, have pity and perform some miracle to show that I am innocent!" His trousers were pulled down for the beating, and lo and behold . . . ! According to the duchess, the Jesuits threw themselves on their knees, saluted the boy's behind with kisses, and assembled the entire school to proclaim a miracle.

One word of command from me is obeyed by millions . . . but I cannot get my three daughters, Pamela, Felicity, and Joan, to come down to breakfast on time.

—Field Marshal Lord Wavell

Edgar Allan Poe was court-martialed from West Point for "gross neglect of duty and disobedience of orders." He failed to show up for parades and classes and he refused to go to church.

George Gershwin was a high school dropout.

To get attention, five-year-old Eleanor Roosevelt deliberately swallowed a penny.

Woodrow Wilson didn't learn to read till he was nine years old. He saw words backward and was probably dyslexic.

Dylan Thomas was just twelve years old when he first had a poem published under his own name. Only it wasn't his poem. The few changes young Dylan made to "His Requiem" included the substitution of his own name for that of the actual author.

Francesco Bernardone was a spoiled rich kid and the leader of a gang of ruffians. He grew up to become Saint Francis of Assisi.

Olympic gymnast Mary Lou Retton described herself as "one of those hyper kids, always jumping up and down on the couch and breaking things."

Percy Bysshe Shelley was so unpopular with the other boys at Eton that they organized a club especially to tease and taunt him.

The École des Beaux Arts turned down Paul Cézanne when he applied for entrance.

In Jack Kennedy's freshman year at Harvard, he got a B in economics and Cs in English, French, and history. His second year was worse: one B, four Cs, and a D.

Jessica Mitford subjected her father to daily "Palsy Practice," by jiggling his elbow as he drank his tea. Jessica explained that this was to prepare him for the palsy that was sure to afflict him a few years hence in his old age. If he became accustomed now to shaking, he wouldn't be forever dropping things later on.

The first half of our lives is ruined by our parents and the second half by our children.

—Clarence Darrow

In 1805, half the student body of Harvard was suspended for rioting over the poor dormitory food.

Children nowadays love luxury, have bad manners, contempt for authority, disrespect for elders . . .

Socrates (469–399 B.C.)

Beethoven's composition teacher pronounced him a hopeless dunce who couldn't learn anything.

Little Mohandas Gandhi was afraid of the dark.

Young Charles Lindbergh had recurrent nightmares of falling through space.

Inventor and philosopher Buckminister Fuller was twice expelled from Harvard—the first time for partying too much, the second (and final) time for "showing no interest in the educational process."

Theodore Roosevelt was described by his mother as looking at birth "like a cross between a terrapin and Dr. Young."

Sensitive little Leo Tolstoy's brothers called him "Lyova Ryova"—Russian for "Leo Cry Baby."

In Ottawa, Illinois, Henry Factly, Jr. was enjoined by a judge from trying to evict his aging mother by (a) putting an electric fence across the drive to shock her;

(b) hiding iron pipes in the grass to trip her; (c) digging up her flower garden; (d) giving a bull a rock-filled milk can to butt in order to make a terrible racket.

Jane Addams, along with five other girls at the Rockford Female Seminary, experimented with opium.

Hamlet is the tragedy of tackling a family problem too soon after college.

—Tom Masson, American writer
and editor (1866–1934)

At the wedding of his Uncle Andrew to Sarah Ferguson, Prince William looked straight at a camera and stuck out his tongue.

William Randolph Hearst was expelled from Harvard for sending his professors chamberpots personalized with their names and photographs.

There are times when parenthood seems nothing but feeding the mouth that bites you.

—Peter De Vries

A Mix of Marriages

There is more to marriage than four bare legs in a bed.

—John Heywood (1497?–1580?)

It destroys one's nerves to be amiable every day to the same human being.

—Benjamin Disraeli

She wondered whether some different set of circumstances might not have resulted in her meeting some different man, and she tried to picture those imaginary circumstances, the life they would have brought her, the unknown other husband. However she imagined him,

29

he wasn't a bit like Charles. He might have been hand-
some, witty, distinguished, magnetic . . .

Madame Bovary
—Gustave Flaubert

There are only about twenty murders a year in London,
and not all are serious. Some are just husbands killing
their wives.

—Cmdr. G. H. Hatherill, British policeman

To impress the servants, Rudyard Kipling's wife insisted
that he dress for dinner in stiff shirt and evening jacket,
even when they dined alone.

Shortly after Grace and Calvin Coolidge were married,
he handed her a large bag filled with socks—fifty-two
pairs of them—that needed mending.

Zsa Zsa Gabor, asked by a talk-show host if she and
her husband of six months, Prince Frederick von An-
hal, had separate bedrooms, replied: ''I've been married most of my life. And when you're married you
don't have sex.''

Count Leo Tolstoy was so outraged when his wife
turned over their infant son to a wet nurse that he wrote
a five-act play, *The Diseased Family*, ridiculing women
too soft and spoiled to nurse their own babies. The

Countess insisted that she'd tried her best to nurse and gave it up only on doctor's orders.

The Marchioness of Blandford was a practical jokester who short-sheeted her husband's bed, made him foam at the mouth by serving him soap sliced to look like cheese, and thought it jolly droll to rig up a pot of ink to fall on his head when he entered a room. One morning the Marquis removed the lid from a silver dish in which he expected to find his bacon and eggs, and found instead a naked baby doll. It was his wife's way of informing him she knew about his illegitimate child.

James Watt, inventor of the steam engine, picked for his second wife a Scottish woman who turned out to be a fanatic housekeeper. She devoted her life to battling dirt, dust, and disorder, which, in her view, included her husband in his grubby leather apron. She made life so miserable for Mr. Watt that he built himself a makeshift kitchen in his workshop. There, amid cylinders and piston rods, he cooked and ate his meals in peace.

When a Cincinnati housewife learned that her husband had betrayed her, she jumped out of a third-story window—and landed on her husband. He was killed. She survived.

I am referred to in that splendid language (Urdu) as "Fella belong Mrs. Queen."

—Prince Philip, Duke of Edinburgh

Walt Disney was fascinated by trains, and argued his wife into signing a contract granting him the legal right to put a miniature railroad in their garden. Mrs. Disney detested the smoky, smelly contraption that toot-tooted around her house all day long.

Every tenth homicide in the United States involves a husband and wife.

You fall in love with someone, and part of what you love about him are the differences between you; and then you get married and the differences start to drive you crazy . . . it seems to me that it's just about impossible to live with someone else.

—Nora Ephron

*It's not so hard to be married.
I've done it two or three times.*

Company
—Lyrics by Stephen Sondheim

In *Upstairs at the White House,* Chief Usher J. B. West quoted Mrs. Nixon's reasons for wanting her own bedroom.

Nobody could sleep with Dick. He wakes up

during the night, switches on the lights, speaks into his tape recorder, or takes notes—it's impossible.

Two weeks after the wedding of Mr. George Bernard Shaw and Miss Charlotte Payne-Townshend, the bridegroom fell downstairs and broke his arm. The accident ruined his expectation for the honeymoon—to write a book on Wagner.

Mrs. Abraham Lincoln was so bad-tempered that her husband secretly paid the maid an extra dollar a week to put up with her.

When Joseph Conrad's wife went into labor, he set out to get the doctor. Told there was no need to hurry, he sat down to breakfast at the doctor's house. A message from Mrs. Conrad urged them to come at once, but it took a second summons to persuade the two men to push back their chairs and get going. Later Conrad termed this conduct unseemly—not his, his wife's.

Sally Kellerman's secret for a happy marriage: "Therapy."

The London *Daily Telegraph* reported that Mrs. Thatcher's husband, Denis, does not much enjoy living at No. 10 Downing Street. The newspaper quoted him telling friends, "My idea of heaven is sitting in my garden on a warm June night with half a bottle of bubbly and my wife in a reasonably relaxed frame of mind.''

John Klepp of Pickett, Wisconsin, angry because his wife went to bed without doing the dishes, burned down the house.

Pianist Clara Schumann wrote in her diary: *My playing is getting all behindhand, as is always the case when Robert is composing. I cannot find one little hour in the day for myself.*

After he had gambled away eight hundred thousand pounds in two years, the Prince of Wales (later George IV) made a deal with his father. He would marry his cousin, Princess Caroline of Brunswick, if his gambling debts were paid from the exchequer. On the wedding night, the bridegroom collapsed in a drunken stupor on the bedroom carpet while his bride awaited him in vain on the nuptial couch beneath a canopy of ostrich plumes. Not surprisingly, the marriage was a disaster.

President Grant refused to allow his wife to have surgery to correct her crossed eyes. He liked them that way.

Asked whether she had ever considered divorce, actress Sybil Thorndike replied, ''Divorce, no. Murder, yes.''

The president loved onions and garlic. Mrs. Eisenhower couldn't bear even the odor, and Rysavy (the White House chef) was torn between their desires. He was ordered by the president to serve a little separate dish of onions on the side, but how could he do that without the odor? Mrs. Eisenhower would say, "I smell onions in my house."
Rysavy left . . .

My Thirty Years Backstairs at the White House
—Lillian Rogers Parks

Clark Gable and Carole Lombard called each other "Ma" and "Pa."

Mrs. Gladstone, wife of the prime minister, always tried to be seated next to her husband at dinner parties. It was, she said, her only chance to talk to him.

For Sophia Loren's fortieth birthday, her husband gave her a gold toilet seat.

Samuel Pepys was caught by his wife embracing Deb, the maid. Mrs. Pepys carried on something awful. She fired Deb, and for weeks kept her husband awake most of the night while she cried and ranted and threatened and reproached. Even so, Mr. Pepys noted jauntily in his diary: *I have laid with my (wife) as a husband more times since this falling out . . . and with more pleasure to her than . . . I think in all the time of our marriage before.*

Peter the Great, less inclined than Mrs. Pepys to let bygones be bygones, had his wife's lover decapitated and his head preserved in a jar of alcohol. The empress had to keep it in her bedroom.

Betty Ford on Gerald Ford: *I can't possibly believe Jerry's a dumb-dumb. He couldn't possibly have been re-elected from the district all these years.*

Pianist-composer-author-and-professional-neurotic Oscar Levant claimed that his marriage worked because "neither of us can stand me."

In a 1952 divorce suit George Bushmire charged that his wife, Celia, put broken glass in his bed, hid his car keys, let the air out of his tires, beat him with her shoes, and tried to poison him. Summing up his wife's behavior, Mr. Bushmire observed, "She didn't cooperate in making our marriage work."

After Lord Chesterfield's marriage to the rich but plain Countess of Walsingham, he took a new mistress, and his wife continued to live with her mother. Lord Chesterfield's only concession to the marriage was to move from Saint James's to Grosvenor Square so he and his wife could be next-door neighbors.

Edith Bunker's complaint: *Archie doesn't know how to worry without getting upset.*

The female weaver bird will have nothing to do with a mate who builds a sloppily woven nest. The rejected male must take the nest apart and completely redo it to meet exacting female standards. Otherwise he is summarily dismissed.

Journalist Dorothy Thompson wrote in her diary: *It was a nice day. Hal* (Sinclair Lewis) *didn't lose his temper with me once.*

Every Sunday Dorothy Parker's father took the family, including his second wife, to the cemetery to visit Dorothy's mother's grave. Mr. Rothschild would intone between sobs into his handkerchief, "We're all here, Eliza! I'm here, Dottie's here, Mrs. Rothschild is here!"

British novelist Evelyn Waugh's wartime letter to his wife:

> *I know you lead a dull life now . . . but that is no reason to make your letters as dull as your life. I simply am not interested in Bridget's children. . . . Don't send me any more of these catalogues of family facts. . . .*

A Parisian woman sued for divorce on the grounds that her husband never gave her Christmas presents. His childhood had been extremely sheltered, and he believed Santa would take care of everything.

"The horror of that moment," the King went on, "I shall never, never forget."
"You will though," said the Queen, "if you don't make a memorandum of it."

Through the Looking Glass
—Lewis Carroll

In *Scoundrel Time* Lillian Hellman recounted the wedding day of Ilo and Henry Wallace, Secretary of Agriculture in the Roosevelt administration. When the young couple emerged from the church, the bridegroom first saw his father's wedding gift. The snazzy new Ford so bedazzled Wallace that he hopped behind the steering wheel and drove off. The guests assured one another that he must be trying out the car to make sure it was safe and comfortable for his bride. An hour passed, then another. Finally, late in the afternoon, the bridegroom returned. "Get in, Ilo, I'd forgotten you!" he called from the driver's seat.

Here lies my wife: here let her lie!
Now she's at rest, and so am I.

—Composed by John Dryden
(1631–1700) as an epitaph
for his wife.

When asked by a guest at a dinner party what she was knitting, Mrs. George Bernard Shaw answered, "Nothing, nothing whatever. It's just that I've heard all those stories of my husband's so many times I have to do something with my hands or I'd choke him."

Marriage is like paying an endless visit in your worst clothes.

—J. B. Priestley

Think you, if Laura had been Petrarch's wife,
He would have written sonnets all his life?

—Lord Byron

Their Lives and Hard Times

My one regret in life is that I am not someone else.

—Woody Allen

If we only wanted to be happy it would be easy; but we want to be happier than other people, which is almost always difficult, since we think them happier than they are.

—Baron de Montesquieu

Martha Washington on her life as First Lady: *I live a very dull life here and know nothing that passes in the town—I never go to any public place—indeed I think I am more like a state prisoner than anything else. . . .*

In his first five years as a professional writer Booth Tarkington made $22.50.

Lucille Ball was fired from the chorus of a road company of *Rio Rita*, and told by a Ziegfeld aide, ''You're not meant for show business. Go home.''

Carmen had a disastrous opening at the Opéra Comique in Paris, and Bizet died believing it a failure.

Sir Edwin Lanseer, nineteenth-century painter and a favorite of Queen Victoria's: *If people only knew as much about painting as I do, they would never buy my paintings*.

When the Prince de Condé was entertaining King Louis XIV at dinner, the fish planned for the first course failed to arrive in time. The chef committed suicide.

In thirty years Huntington Hartford reduced the $90 million A&P fortune he inherited to a mere $8.7 million or so. His bad investments included an art museum, a magazine, a resort, a theater, and several ex-wives.

Where's my balloon and what's that small piece of damp rag doing?

Winnie-the-Pooh
A. A. Milne

During all the years the Trumans lived in Washington, Mrs. Truman couldn't find a laundry that met her standards. Sheets and pillowcases were sent home to Kansas City to be laundered, and the president washed his own underwear.

When John Ruskin wrote a derogatory review of Whistler's paintings, Whistler sued for libel and won. But he received only a farthing in damages, and the cost of the trial ruined Whistler financially. He was forced to sell his house and his porcelain collection.

Doug Sanders had only to make a one-and-a-half-foot putt to win the 1970 British Open. He missed, forcing a playoff with Jack Nicklaus, who subsequently won the tournament.

Flaubert became so weary of criticism of *Madame Bovary*, he wished he could "buy up every copy and throw them all into the fire and never hear of the book again."

When President and Mrs. Benjamin Harrison moved into the White House, they brought with them a family of eleven: a son and daughter, their spouses and three children, Mrs. Harrison's eighty-nine-year-old father, and her widowed niece. The White House in 1889 had one bathroom.

Charles Lamb's play, *Mr. H——*, was hissed offstage by the audience. Fearful he might be recognized as the author, Lamb joined in the hissing.

My whole life is a movie. It's just that there are no dissolves. I have to live through every agonizing moment of it. My life needs editing.

—Mort Sahl

Schubert's compositions earned him less than three thousand dollars in his thirty-one years of life. The highest price he was paid for a song was less than fifteen dollars; for some he received twenty cents.

Rudyard Kipling was fired from his first job as a reporter for the San Francisco *Examiner* and told he didn't know how to use the English language.

Princess Michael of Kent, whose husband is Queen Elizabeth's cousin, admits she is "bored rigid" with the public appearances she must make as a member of the royal family.

President Harding told a White House visitor, "I knew this job would be too much for me."

Mata Hari, who considered her breasts not sufficiently voluptuous, refused to let her lovers see them. When asked why not, she told a well-rehearsed story that her husband had bitten off her nipples.

As soon as James Garfield was elected president, he began having nightmares of being naked and lost.

Asked if she had any enemies, Dinah Shore replied, "*I'm* not crazy about me."

My verses are no damn good.

—Dorothy Parker

My vigor, vitality, and cheek repel me. I am the kind of woman I would run away from.

—Lady Astor

You ever see my act? You could give me every good line since Chaucer, and I'd ruin it.

—Zeppo Marx

Scott Fitzgerald was convinced his penis was abnormally small until Ernest Hemingway took him on an art museum tour of nude statues and showed him it wasn't so.

Michelangelo's answer to Pope Julius's complaint that he was taking too long to paint the Sistine Chapel ceiling: "I *told* your Holiness I was no painter."

In my own mind, I am still that fat brunette from Toledo, and I always will be.

—Gloria Steinem

Norman Vincent Peale threw out the manuscript of *The Power of Positive Thinking* because it seemed to him no good. His wife rescued it.

According to a survey published in 1985 by *Better Homes and Gardens*, nearly ninety per cent of Americans think they weigh too much.

Alec Guinness: *I'm very insecure about my work. I've never done anything I couldn't pull to bits.*

To be human is to feel oneself inferior.

—Alfred Adler, German psychoanalyst

Along with other young revolutionaries, Fyodor Dostoyevski was tried for conspiracy and sentenced to death by firing squad. Preparations were made for the execution, and the prisoners were lined up to be shot. While they braced themselves in excruciating suspense for the volley of gunfire that would end their lives, a roll of drums beat retreat and the firing squad lowered their rifles. The stunned prisoners were read a pardon from Czar Nicholas that commuted the sentences of death to imprisonment. It had been the czar's order that the sham execution be dragged out to the last possible moment. The ordeal aggravated Dostoyevski's epilepsy, and he suffered severe seizures the rest of his life.

Anybody can be Pope; the proof is that I have become one.

—Pope John XXIII

I don't enjoy being Malcolm Sargent.

—Malcolm Sargent, British conductor

Gorgeous film star Nastassia Kinski describes her breasts as too small and her bottom too big.

> *The tumult and the shouting dies;*
> *The Captains and the Kings depart.*
> *Still stands Thine ancient sacrifice,*
> *An humble and a contrite heart.*
> *Lord God of Hosts, be with us yet,*
> *Lest we forget—lest we forget!*

Kipling wrote *Recessional* and tossed it into the wastepaper basket. It was retrieved by a friend who insisted it be published.

I'm as pure as the driven slush.

—Tallulah Bankhead

Sigmund Freud's description of himself at a party: *I fit in no better than the cholera would have.*

Cézanne thought so little of his paintings he often gave them to his small son to cut up for jigsaw puzzles.

William Howard Taft weighed 332 pounds when he was president. He kept getting stuck in the White House bathtub until an outsized one was installed.

Edgar Rice Burroughs, who wrote *Tarzan of the Apes*, didn't think it was much of a story and doubted that anyone would read it.

Although Thomas Jefferson kept precise account books, crop failures and family obligations sunk him deeper and deeper into debt. At his death he owed $107,274. Monticello had to be sold and its furnishings auctioned.

Surinam, a tiny South American country, entered the Olympics for the first time in 1960. It sent one athlete, Wim Essajas, to compete in the 800-meter track event. Wim slept through the trials, thereby making his country ineligible for the competition.

P. G. Wodehouse: *I am a mass of diffidence and I-wonder-if-this-is-going-to-be-all-right-ness, and I envy those tough, square-jawed authors, smoking pipes and talking out of the side of their mouths, who are perfectly confident, every time they start a new book, that it will be a masterpiece.*

It is eleven years since I have seen my figure in a glass. The last reflection I saw there was so disagreeable, I resolved to spare myself such mortification in the future.

—Lady Mary Wortley Montague (1757)

It's not what you'd call a figure, is it?

—Twiggy

I am a man of reserved, cold, and forbidding manners.

—John Quincy Adams

O what a rogue and peasant slave am I.

—Hamlet

Eeyore, the old Grey Donkey, stood by the side of the stream and looked at himself in the water.
"Pathetic," he said. "That's what it is. Pathetic."

Winnie-the-Pooh
—A. A. Milne

I have offended God and mankind because my work didn't reach the quality it should have.

—Leonardo da Vinci

I'm exactly as I appear. There is no warm, lovable person inside. Beneath my cold exterior, once you break the ice, you find cold water.

—Gore Vidal

Modigliani's only show in his lifetime (1884–1920) was closed by police for indecency because it included paintings of nude women.

I hate to see myself on the screen. I hate the way I look. I hate the sound of my voice. I'm always thinking I should have played it better.

—Elizabeth Taylor

". . . a flat failure. . . .": President Lincoln's opinion of his address at Gettysburg.

Deep down I'm pretty superficial.

—Ava Gardner

A letter from a publisher to Zane Grey:

> *You've wasted enough of our time with your junk. You can't write, you never could write, and you will never be able to write.*

Were it not for frustration and humiliation,
I suppose the human race would get ideas above its station.

—Ogden Nash

Some Bunch of Relatives

I think my father (Dore Schary, head of MGM) . . .
*and the rest of them invented the happy family and put
it into movies to drive everyone crazy.*

—Jill Robinson

Cesare Borgia didn't let family ties interfere with opportunities. He had the Duke of Bisceglie murdered for political purposes, even though the young duke was the adored husband of his sister Lucrezia. Cesare also masterminded the murder of the Duke of Gandia, who happened to be his brother Giovanni.

The Duke of Windsor penned his opinion of his kinfolk in a letter to Wallis Warfield Simpson written shortly after he had abdicated as King Edward VIII:

> *God, how I hate and despise the lot. I hope one day to, and I mean to, get back at those swine and at least make them realize how disgustingly and unsportingly they have behaved.*

Lyndon Johnson's younger brother, Sam Houston, had a predilection for bad checks and booze. To prevent embarrassing incidents during his presidency, Lyndon kept Sam under virtual house arrest on the third floor of the White House.

Edith Sitwell, in a letter to Cecil Beaton, wrote of meeting Picasso:

> *He is a delightful, kindly, friendly, simple little man, and one would know him for a great man anywhere. At the moment, he was extremely excited and overjoyed because his mother-in-law had just died . . . and he was looking forward to the funeral . . .*

Catherine the Great was outraged by the French fashions her daughter-in-law brought back from a European tour. Untouched by Maria Feodorovna's tears, the empress ordered the Parisian fripperies sent back.

Nature ordains friendship with relatives, but it is never very stable.

—Cicero

Lewis DuPont Smith, twenty-eight-year-old heir to a $1.5-million slice of the DuPont Chemical fortune and a convert to the politics of Lyndon H. LaRouche, Jr., handed over $212,000 to the organization. The family went to court to have Lewis declared incompetent. He denounced his father and grandfather as "oligarchs," accused his mother of killing his maternal grandmother, who died of pneumonia, and charged that his family was trying to take away his constitutional rights because he proposed to spend his money in "some fashion other than the obscene way . . . they spend theirs."

Evelyn Waugh's diary: *There has arrived in the house one Emma Raban, a half sister to my mother, who makes life very heavy to me. I cannot write or think, I hate her so.*

Patrick Reynolds, an heir to the R. J. Reynolds tobacco fortune, is an antismoking activist.

John Paul Getty, the richest man in the world and a dedicated tightwad, refused for five months to ransom his kidnapped grandson. It wasn't until the young man's ear arrived in the mail, along with a note from the kidnappers threatening next to send his cut-up body, that his grandfather parted with the $3.2 million demanded to free him.

Smack in the middle of Virginia and Leonard Woolf's wedding ceremony, Virginia's self-centered sister Vanessa interrupted to ask what steps she should take to change the name of her second son. "One thing at a time," the registry clerk chided her, "one thing at a time."

Sigmund Freud on his future mother-in-law: . . . *I can foresee more than one opportunity of making myself disagreeable to her, and I don't mean to avoid them.*

Benson Ford, during a bitter and unsuccessful battle to get a seat on the Ford Motor Company board left vacant by his father's death, arrived at a family meeting at his Uncle Henry's Grosse Pointe house wearing a hidden microphone. It was detected by electronic surveillance equipment installed in the house.

In the seventeenth century, the Marquise de Brinvilliers and her lover killed off her father by dosing him with poison for eight grueling months. In the same painstaking fashion, they did away with her two brothers. Then they started to work on her husband. Lucky for the Marquis, his wife's lover was no longer sure he wanted to marry such a merciless woman but was understandably disinclined to tell her so. Instead, for every dose of poison the Marquise gave her husband, the lover sneaked an antidote into him. The Marquis consequently survived, but with a considerably worse-for-wear liver.

I was in Washington recently, and Jimmy was buying four new suits. As tight as Jimmy is, he wouldn't be buying new suits if he wasn't going to run again.

—President Carter's brother Billy

Another of Billy's witticisms: *Jimmy's around too many people that kiss his ass all the time.*

Thomas Jefferson's granddaughter, Anne, married Charles Lewis Bankhead, a handsome member of a distinguished family, who beat her. When Anne's brother, Thomas Jefferson Randolph, accused Bankhead of abusing his sister, his brother-in-law stabbed him.

It's no wonder Donald Duck was so high-strung. Look at the family he had to put up with:

—His diabolical nephews, Huey, Dewey, and Louie, whose terrorist tactics kept Donald in a perpetual swivet;

—His sister, Dumbella, who sent Huey, Dewey, and Louie to Unca Duck for a never-ending visit;

—Donald's gluttonous and insensitive cousin, Gus Goose;

—His miserly and cantankerous Uncle Scrooge McDuck, who knew the date on every dime of his three cubic acres of money;

—Gladstone Gander, his chiseling bum of a cousin; and

—Grandma Duck, a prude who strongly disapproved of Donald's coquettish girlfriend, Daisy.

George Whitman on his brother Walt's book, *Leaves of Grass: I saw the book, but I didn't read it at all—didn't think it worth reading.* . . .

If a man's character is to be abused, there's nobody like a relative to do the business.

—William Makepeace Thackerey

The golden eagle usually lays two eggs several days apart. The older and larger chick customarily kills its younger sibling to avoid having to share food with it.

Samuel Pepys invited his maiden sister, Paulina, to live at his house, not as a guest but a servant. Paulina was not permitted to sit at table with her brother and his wife. She left in tears after a few months.

In May, 1986, *The Louisville Courier-Journal* and *Louisville Times*, owned by the patrician Bingham family of Louisville, Kentucky, were sold to the Gannett Company for an estimated three hundred million dollars. Chairman of the board Barry Bingham, Sr., explained the sale, saying, "There was no other way out of the emotional tangle we'd fallen into." The siblings had taken to flinging at one another words like "betrayal!" "irrational!" and "sexist!"

In a letter to her daughter Vicky, Queen Victoria expressed her opinion of her daughter-in-law Princess Alexandra: *I am sorry for Bertie. I don't think she makes his home comfortable; she is never ready for breakfast—not being out of her room till eleven often, and poor Bertie breakfasts alone. . . .*

After living twenty-six years with her daughter Bess and family, Madge Gates Wallace still called her son-in-law, Harry, "Mr. Truman." She was heard to remark in his presence that other men would have made a better president, including "that nice man, Thomas E. Dewey."

At the age of thirty-seven, Russian poet Alexander Pushkin was mortally wounded in a duel with his wife's lover, Baron Georges d'Anthes, who also happened to be her sister's husband.

Richard Nixon's brother, Donald, had a proclivity for shady financial deals. When Nixon was president, he kept track of Donald by having his telephone tapped by the Secret Service.

. . . my Aunt Agatha has a fairly fruity reputation as a hostess. But then, I take it she doesn't ballyrag her other guests the way she does me. I don't think I can remember a single meal with her since I was a kid of tender years at which she didn't turn the conversation sooner or later to the subject of my frightfulness.

—P. G. Wodehouse

In vino veritas:

Sam Sebastiani was booted out as president of the forty-million-dollar family business (Sebastiani Vineyards) by his mother, brother, and sister. He countered by opening a rival vineyard.

Joseph Gallo opened a cheese factory and was sued by his brothers, Ernest and Julio (E&J Gallo Winery), for infringing on the Gallo trademark. Joseph countersued his brothers for a one-third interest in their winery, which he contended was his rightful inheritance.

Only thirty percent of family businesses survive their founders and make it into the second generation.

Miss Bingley's congratulations to her brother on his approaching marriage were all that was affectionate and insincere.

—Pride and Prejudice
Jane Austen

Winston Churchill's mother, Jennie, on her relationship with her mother-in-law, the Duchess of Marlborough: *We are always studiously polite to each other, but it is rather like a volcano ready to burst out at any moment.*

Lord Byron's frequently expressed reason for not blowing his brains out: *It would have given pleasure to my mother-in-law.*

Lillian Carter complained that her son Jimmy paid more attention to his wife than to his mother.

> *One would be in less danger*
> *From the wiles of a stranger*
> *If one's own kin and kith*
> *Were more fun to be with.*
>
> —Ogden Nash

Sundry Sex Lives

If you compare your sex life to the frolics that reputedly occur in the vast beds of Saudi Arabian billionaires, or to the goings-on pictured in Calvin Klein perfume ads, your own liaisons may strike you as singularly tepid. But don't tear off in a panic to consult a sex therapist. Not everyone pranks it up beneath a mirrored ceiling. There are quite a number of wallflowers at the orgy.

A U.S. Government study of five thousand married men revealed them to be considerably less fixated on sex than their counterparts in John Updike novels. Asked to name the single most important thing in their lives, seventy-five percent said, "My job."

A 1978 survey conducted by the *Journal of Sexual Research* asked women to choose between a good book and sex with their husbands. Two out of three opted for the book.

Sir Isaac Newton's sex life was apparently nonexistent. He was so absorbed in mathematical equations he quite possibly didn't notice that something was missing.

Hans Christian Andersen died a virgin at the age of seventy, a state of no affairs he blamed on his gangling appearance. A more likely impediment was his habit of falling in love only with women who hadn't the least interest in him.

Nineteenth-century writer John Ruskin was flabbergasted into permanent celibacy on his wedding night by the sight of his wife naked. Unlike marble statues he admired, she had pubic hair.

Josephine complained that Napoleon went at it ''like a fireman tackling a fire.''

The male paper nautilus leaves his penis inside the female after mating and must wait until he grows a new one to repeat the performance.

Tallulah Bankhead grumbled: *I've tried several varieties of sex. The conventional position makes me claustrophobic. And the others give me a stiff neck or lockjaw.*

The male drone bumblebee has one brief fling with the queen, and that's the end of it. Not the end of the bee's sex life. The end of the bee.

Country singer Loretta Lynn bemoaned female anatomy: *Really that little dealybob is too far away from the hole. It should be built right in. . . .*

Cosmopolitan editor Helen Gurley Brown defended sex as "pretty terrific." Even so, she rated it second to good food.

Eating also won over sex in a 1986 survey reported in the Boston *Globe*. The study showed that most Americans would choose dinner in a good restaurant over sex with anyone.

I don't know whether you've ever had a woman eat an apple while you were doing it . . . well, you can imagine how that affects you.

Tropic of Capricorn
—Henry Miller

The male balloon fly brings a gift of prey to the female, who becomes so engrossed with it she does not notice that she is being mated.

The Animal Family
—Philip Whitfield

The female (of species other than homo sapiens) *does not appear to experience any kind of climax. If there is anything that could be called an orgasm, it is a trivial response when compared with that of the female of our own species.*

The Naked Ape
—Desmond Morris

In *American Couples*, a survey of relationships by Philip Blumstein and Pepper Schwartz, an unnamed woman cooly placed sex in her scheme of things: *I don't equate it with a sale at Bloomingdale's. That I could do all the time. But it's not like going to the dentist, either. It's between the two extremes. Closer to Bloomingdale's than to the dentist.*

Some things are better than sex and some are worse, but there's nothing else like it.

—W. C. Fields

Sophia Loren, asked why she had not mentioned Peter Sellers as one of her lovers in her autobiography, said, "I only wrote about things that were important to me."

The Duke of Wellington was singled out by a courtesan, Harriett Wilson, as "the most unentertaining of all my lovers."

Helen Lawrenson, who wrote *Latins Are Lousy Lovers*, vouchsafed that Bernard Baruch, though not Latin, still qualified.

Despite its reputation as a lecherous beast, the male gorilla has a tiny penis and isn't much interested in sex.

The human male has the largest penis of any primate.

The Naked Ape
—Desmond Morris

Sigmund Freud—of all people—prudishly forbade his wife to visit a friend who had, as Mrs. Freud put it, "married before her wedding."

Clark Gable had a voluminous sex life (he'd go to bed with almost anyone simply because she was there), but his performance was said to be perfunctory.

If I have to cry, I think of my sex life. If I have to laugh, I think of my sex life.

—Glenda Jackson

I wish I had as much in bed as I get in the newspapers.

—Linda Ronstadt

They're doing things on the screen nowadays that I wouldn't even do in bed.

—Bob Hope

They Never Heard
of Calories

Participants in a 1986 *People* magazine poll rated over-eating a worse sin than smoking, failing to vote, or reading pornography.

Brillat-Savarin's Breakfast

Two Dozen Oysters
Broiled Kidneys
Foie Gras
Truffle Pie
Fondue
Fruit
Sweetmeats
Liqueurs

President Taft's Lunch

Salmon Cutlets with Peas
Roast Tenderloin of Beef
Roast Turkey
Cold Tongue
Cold Ham
Vegetable Salad
Potato Salad
Frozen Pudding
Cake
Fruit
Coffee

Louis XIV's Dinner

Four Plates of Different Soups
A Whole Pheasant
A Whole Partridge
Two Great Slices of Ham
A Large Dish of Salad
Mutton with Gravy and Garlic
Pastry
Fruit
Hard-Boiled Eggs

Mole, Badger, Rat, and Toad's Midnight Snack

Cold Chicken
Tongue
Lobster Salad
French Rolls and Butter
Guava Jelly
Cheese
Celery
Trifle

The Wind in the Willows
—Kenneth Grahame

Ichabod Crane's Daydream

In his devouring mind's eye, he pictured to himself every roasting-pig running about with a pudding in his belly, and an apple in his mouth; the pigeons were snugly put to bed in a comfortable pie, and tucked in with a coverlet of crust; the geese were swimming in their own gravy; and the ducks pairing cosily in dishes, like snug married couples . . .

As Ichabod jogged slowly on his way, he beheld great fields of Indian corn with its golden ears peeping from their leafy coverts, and holding out the promise of cakes and hasty pudding; and the yellow pumpkins lying beneath them, turning up in pies; and anon he passed the fragrant buckwheat fields, breathing the odor of the beehive; and as he beheld them, soft anticipations stole over his mind of dainty slapjacks, well buttered and garnished with honey or treacle . . .

"The Legend of Sleepy Hollow"
—Washington Irving

Lunch on William Vanderbilt's Yacht

Oeufs à l'Aurore
Langouste à la Newburg
Tournedos à la Moelle
Pommes de Terre   Épinards
Asperges   Sauce Hollandaise
Petit Poulet Grillé au Cresson
Salade
Crêpes aux Confitures
Café et Dessert

Eugene Gant's Icebox Raid

Well, perhaps I'll have a slice or two of that pink Austrian ham . . . and yes, perhaps, I'll have a slice of this roast beef . . . say a slice of red rare meat there at the center, with just a trifle of that crisp brown crackling . . . and a little of that cold but brown . . . gravy . . . and a slice of that plump chicken—some white meat . . . a spoonful or two of those lima beans . . . a tomato slice or two, a speared forkful of those thin-sliced cucumbers . . . a little corn perhaps, a bottle of this milk, a pound of butter and that crusty loaf of bread . . .

Of Time and the River
—Thomas Wolfe

A Tammany Hall Banquet Hosted in 1899 at the Waldolf-Astoria by Randolph Guggenheimer

Clusters of Hamburg Grapes
Canapés
Small Bluepoint Oysters
Lemardelais à la Princesse
Green Turtle Soup
Amontillado
Lobster
Broiled Boned Delaware River Shad
Columbine of Chicken
Crown Roast of Mountain Sheep
Chestnut Purée
Brussels Sprouts Sauté
New Asparagus
Cream Sauce and Vinaigrette
Champagne
Diamondback Terrapin

Crême de Menthe Sherbet
Canvasback Duck
Orange and Grapefruit Salad
Fresh Strawberries
Blue Raspberries
Vanilla Mousse
Fresh Fruits
Bonbons   Walnuts   Coffee
Vintage 1811 Cognac

A gourmet who thinks of calories is like a tart who looks at her watch.

—James Beard

Worse Luck

Failing to win the lottery does not qualify as bad luck, no matter how many tickets you bought and however urgently you need that jackpot. Bad luck is when something awful that should not (according to all reasonable expectations) happen, happens.

In Jacksonville, the Riverside Chevrolet Company launched a sales campaign featuring the slogan "Look for it! Something big is going to happen!" A few hours later the showroom ceiling collapsed on six new cars.

Aeschylus was killed by a tortoise dropped by an eagle that mistook his bald head for a rock. So they say.

At a dinner party, the large belt buckle on Mrs. George S. Kaufman's dress hooked itself onto the lace table-cloth, a happenstance she failed to observe. When the guests adjourned to the drawing room, Mrs. Kaufman was followed by the cloth, which took with it a clattering tumble of china, silver, ashtrays, centerpiece, and after-dinner mints.

Fernande Olivier lived with Picasso for seven years when he was young and poor. She was not impressed with his paintings, which included many portraits of her she thought unflattering. In 1912 she moved out and took with her a little heart-shaped mirror as her only memento of the years with her Spanish painter. Fernande never saw Picasso again, and she died in poverty in 1966. A few years after her death, a cubist painting of her by Picasso sold in London for $790,000.

In Pacific Beach, California, a man lost a wheel off his trailer. He watched it roll into the hands of a stranger, who loaded it into his car and drove off.

Had careless burglars not left a strip of tape over a door latch in the basement garage of a Washington, D.C. office complex, a suspicious night watchman would not have taken the first step that led twenty-six months later to the resignation of Richard Nixon.

With a revolutionary mob close behind them, Louis XVI, Marie Antoinette, and their family fled Paris in disguise. They might have escaped but for a narrow bridge outside Chantrix. When one of the carriage wheels bumped against its side, the horses reared and broke the harness. The hour lost in repairs gave the mob time to catch up and haul the royal family back to Paris, where they were tried for treason and sent to the guillotine.

By going a few minutes sooner or later, by stopping to speak with a friend on the corner, by meeting this man or that, or by turning down this street instead of the other, we may let slip some impending evil, by which the whole current of our lives would have been changed. There is no possible solution in the dark enigma but the one word "Providence."

—Henry Wadsworth Longfellow

A man who survived a trip over Niagara Falls in a barrel later skidded on a banana peel and died of complications from the fall.

Thomas Carlyle loaned the manuscript of his history of the French Revolution to his friend, John Stuart Mill. A housemaid used the manuscript to light a fire. Carlyle had to rewrite the book from memory.

More than one hundred people died when fire raged through a Tokyo department store in November 1973. The sprinkler system wasn't working that day; it was being overhauled for Fire Prevention Week.

If Lt. Col. Douglas Stewart had not had a sudden impulse to buzz over in his Piper Cub to have tea with friends in Buckinghamshire, the perpetrators of England's brilliantly executed seven-million-dollar train robbery might have got away with it. The robbers, who were hiding out in an isolated farm house twenty miles from the scene of the crime, spotted the Cub overhead. Certain it must be the police, they panicked and fled, leaving damning evidence and fingerprints everywhere.

Napoleon's constipation may have cost him the Battle of Waterloo. His advance of the French armies had caught the English unprepared. A swift attack would likely have finished them. But Napoleon's digestive problems made him late to the battlefield on the crucial morning of June 17. The delay gave the Duke of Wellington time to muster his forces, and the Prussians to come to his aid.

A good-looking young drummer named Pete Best spent two years with a struggling English rock group. Hundreds of his adoring fans protested when he was replaced by a drummer named Ringo Starr. During the next twenty-four months, the Beatles grossed forty million dollars. Pete Best made eight pounds a week slicing bread in a bakery.

In 1982 Bill Curtis, an electronic technician at the Vancouver airport, became convinced that a third world war was about to erupt. Casting about for a safe place to move his family, he chose a remote British protectorate in the South Atlantic, inhabited by seven hundred thousand sheep and eighteen hundred British subjects. In September the Curtises sold everything and moved with their two children to the Falkland Islands. The next April four thousand Argentinian troops attacked to claim the islands for Argentina. Over the next three months, the peace-seeking Curtises were subjected to bombings, curfews, blackouts, looting, shelling, and antiaircraft fire.

In Manteno, Illinois, Edward Gortman bought a farm at 4:30 P.M. At 5:30 P.M. he watched a tornado level it.

> *Everything is 60–40 against.*
> —Satchel Paige

Bernard Cabanes, editor of Agence France Presse, and Bernard Cabanes, editor of *Le Parisien Libéré*, a daily newspaper, were continually mistaken for each other. Minutes after the head of the news agency was killed in the doorway of his apartment by a bomb explosion, an anonymous phone caller claimed credit for having blown up the newspaper editor.

Auto thieves in Southern Rhodesia, afraid they'd be heard starting the engine of a car they were stealing, pushed it half a mile in the dark before they discovered its engine had been removed for repairs.

As a spy for the French in World War I, Mata Hari was so ineffectual her employers thought she must be working as a counterspy for the Germans. In a fair trial it would have become obvious that her failure to extract secrets from German officers resulted from incompetence rather than cunning. But Mata Hari's trial as a counterespionage agent was a frame-up. The French government wanted a conviction to bolster support for the war, and the already-notorious Mata Hari (she performed striptease masquerading as Oriental mysticism) was a made-to-order scapegoat. She was a silly, self-centered woman with grandiose delusions, but it was unlikely she deserved to be shot as a German spy.

Making an escape from Toronto police, a housebreaker leaped over a fence and landed on a skunk. Police had no trouble tracking him down.

When radioactivity reached a threatening level at the nuclear plant in Sellafield, England, the Merlin family was forced to move. They went to Cumbria in northern England and started a new life as sheep farmers. In May 1986 their flock was contaminated by radioactive clouds that had drifted there from the Soviet nuclear disaster at Chernobyl.

I have suffered misery—suffered it through unwitting deeds, and of those acts—be Heaven my witness!—no part was of mine own choice.

Oedipus at Colonus
—Sophocles

It took three blows of the ax to sever the head of Mary, Queen of Scots. When the executioner held up her head by its long auburn hair and cried, "God Save the Queen!" the head fell to the ground. Mary had been wearing a wig. Spectators were stunned to see that her own hair was gray and short.

Jim knowed all kinds of signs. He said he knowed most everything. I said it looked to me like all the signs was about bad luck, and so I asked him if there warn't any good-luck signs. He says: "Mighty few—and dey ain't no use to a body. What you want to know when good luck's a comin for? Want to keep it off?"

The Adventures of Huckleberry Finn
—Mark Twain

If Shakespeare had not mentioned starlings in *Henry IV, Part One*, the United States would today be free of the little nuisances. Starlings were imported in the 1890s by a well-meaning philanthropist whose mission it was to populate the U.S. with all the birds mentioned in Shakespeare's works.

*They call you "Lady Luck"
But there is room for doubt.
At times you have a very un-
ladylike way of running out.*

Guys and Dolls
Lyrics by Frank Loesser

Insults, Put-Downs and Nasty Cracks

. . . from envy, hatred, and malice and from all uncharitableness, Good Lord, deliver us.

—The Book of Common Prayer

Praise, like gold and diamonds, owes its value only to scarcity.

—Samuel Johnson

The Chicago *Times*'s verdict on President Lincoln's address at Gettysburg in 1863: *. . . silly, flat, and dishwatery utterances . . .*

The Odessa *Courier* on *Anna Karenina*: "Sentimental rubbish."

Leonardo da Vinci bores me. He ought to have stuck to his flying machines.

—Auguste Renoir

The more I read Socrates, the less I wonder why they poisoned him.

—Thomas Macauley

Liszt can't squeeze from his brain the least morsel of any merit.

—Frédéric Chopin

John Adams described George Washington as "an old mutton-head."

Tolstoy to Chekhov: *Shakespeare's plays are bad enough, but yours are worse.*

Film director Otto Preminger's view of Marilyn Monroe: *A vacuum with nipples.*

Asked if he knew George Moore, Oscar Wilde answered: "*Know* him? I know him so well that I haven't spoken to him for ten years."

W. Somerset Maugham's size-up of Winston Churchill: *If you think I'm gaga, you should see Winston.*

Poet Anna de Noailles' Gallic view of her meeting with Sigmund Freud: *Surely he never wrote his "sexy" books. What a terrible man. I am sure he has never been unfaithful to his wife. It's quite abnormal and scandalous.*

Henry James on Anthony Trollope: . . . *the dullest Briton of them all*.

William Faulkner on Henry James: . . . *the nicest old lady I ever met*.

Evelyn Waugh's response to a good report about Randolph Churchill's surgery: *A typical triumph of modern science to find the only part of Randolph that was not malignant and remove it.*

If all men knew what each said of the other, there would not be four friends in the world.

—Pascal

How can I talk to a fellow (Woodrow Wilson) *who thinks himself the first man in two thousand years to know anything about peace on earth?*

—Georges Clemenceau

Nietzsche wrote to a rival in love: *I should very much like to give you a lesson in practical morality with the help of a few bullets.*

Nixon is the kind of politician who would cut down a redwood tree, then mount the stump and make a speech for conservation.

—Adlai Stevenson

Tolstoy on Wagner's *Siegfried: It was all so stupid I had difficulty seeing it out.*

The cruelest thing that has happened to Lincoln since Booth was to fall into the hands of Carl Sandburg.

—Critic Edmund Wilson's verdict on Sandburg's biography of Lincoln

Tallulah Bankhead barged down the Nile last night as Cleopatra—and sank.

—Drama critic John Mason Brown's review of *Antony and Cleopatra*

A behind-her-back name for Prime Minister Margaret Thatcher: Attila the Hen.

John Adams' sniffy put-down of Aaron Burr: *The bastard son of a Scotch peddler.*

One thing I learned above all else from Margaret Bourke-White is the kind of woman I didn't want to be.

—Peggy Sargent, secretary to
photographer Bourke-White

Ernest Hemingway's writing reminds me of the farting of an old horse.

—E. B. White

William McKinley has no more backbone than a chocolate éclair.

—Theodore Roosevelt

A publisher who rejected Proust's *Swann's Way* wrote: *I simply cannot understand why a gentleman should take thirty pages to describe how he turned round and round in his bed before he could get to sleep.*

George S. Kaufman's sentiments toward theatrical producer Jed Harris: *When I die, I want to be cremated and have my ashes thrown in Jed Harris's face.*

H. L. Mencken to George Bernard Shaw: *The more I think you over, the more it comes home to me what an unmitigated Middle Victorian ass you are!*

Calvin Coolidge looked as if he had been weaned on a pickle.

—Alice Roosevelt Longworth

George Washington is too illiterate, unread, and unlearned for his station and reputation.

—John Adams

Adlai Stevenson was a man who could never make up his mind whether he had to go to the bathroom or not.

—Harry Truman

In his 1968 list of Worst Dressed Women, the designer known as "Mr. Blackwell" described Elizabeth Taylor as looking like "two small boys fighting underneath a mink blanket."

There is absolutely nothing wrong with Oscar Levant that a miracle cannot fix.

—Alexander Woollcott

Horace Walpole called poet Lady Mary Wortley Montagu "an old, foul, tawdry, painted, plastered personage."

Horace Walpole called feminist Mary Wollstonecraft "a hyena in skirts."

Russian poet Yevgeny Yevtushenko called Barbara Walters, who interviewed him, "a hyena in syrup."

Dwight D. Eisenhower on General Douglas MacArthur: *Oh, yes, I studied dramatics under him for twelve years.*

I don't see why Walter Winchell is allowed to live.

—Ethel Barrymore

> *There's something in a stupid ass,*
> *And something in a heavy dunce*
>   *But never since I went to school*
>   *I heard or so saw so damn'd a fool*
> *As William Wordsworth is for once. . . .*

—Lord Byron

W. H. Auden's sum-up of Edgar Allan Poe: *. . . an unmanly sort of man whose love-life seems to have been largely confined to crying in laps and playing house.*

The president (Abraham Lincoln) is nothing more than a well-meaning baboon.

—General George McClellan

So Evelyn Waugh is in his coffin. Died of snobbery.

—Cecil Beaton

King George II on Shakespeare: *I cannot read him; he is such a bombast fellow.*

Dorothy Kilgallen is the only woman I wouldn't mind my wife catching me with . . . I don't know why she took such umbrage at my comments on birth control, she's such a living argument for it.

—Johnny Carson

Lloyd George couldn't see a belt without hitting below it.

—Lady Margot Asquith

The affair between Margot Asquith and Margot Asquith will live as one of the prettiest love stories of all literature.

—Dorothy Parker

Handel claimed that his cook was a better musician than Gluck.

Tchaikovsky's opinion of Brahms: *What a giftless bastard.*

Thomas E. Dewey is just about the nastiest little man I've ever known. He struts sitting down.

—Mrs. Clarence Dykstra

One must have a heart of stone to read the death of little Nell without laughing.

—Oscar Wilde on Dickens's *Old Curiosity Shop*

That two thousand years after Alexander the Great and Julius Caesar, a man like Ulysses S. Grant should be called . . . the highest product of the most advanced evolution, made evolution ludicrous . . .

—Henry Adams

Tennis ace Rosemary Casals on Bobby Riggs: *He can't hear, can't see, walks like a duck, and is an idiot besides.*

Zachary Taylor is dead and gone to hell, and I am glad of it.

—Govenor Brigham Young of the Utah Territory

Norman Mailer said of Jacqueline Kennedy's televised tour of the White House that she walked through the program *"like a starlet who is utterly without talent."*

Writer S. J. Perelman's view of Groucho Marx: . . . *the compassion of an icicle, the effrontery of a carnival shill, and the generosity of a pawnbroker.*

When in good humour Queen Anne was meekly stupid, and when in bad humour was sulkily stupid.

— *T.B. Macaulay*

The reason so many people showed up at Louis B. Mayer's funeral was because they wanted to make sure he was dead.

—Samuel Goldwyn

If Gladstone fell into the Thames, that would be a misfortune, and if anybody pulled him out that would be a calamity.

—Benjamin Disraeli

The last part of it (James Joyce's Ulysses) is the dirtiest, most indecent, most obscene thing ever written. Yes, it is . . . it is filthy.

—D. H. Lawrence

The *Sunday Chronicle*'s verdict on *Lady Chatterly's Lover* by D. H. Lawrence: . . . *one of the most filthy and abominable books ever written . . . reeking with obscenity and lewdness . . .*

Coolidge's chief feat was to sleep more than any other president.

—H. L. Mencken

George Bernard Shaw to Joseph Conrad: *You know, my dear fellow, your books won't do.*

A glorified bandmaster!

—Sir Thomas Beecham on Arturo Toscanini

Plato is a bore.

—Nietzsche

I much prefer praise, insincere or not, to sincere criticism.

—Plautus

There's a lot to be said for being nouveau riche, and the Reagans mean to say it all.

—Gore Vidal

Poor Matt (Matthew Arnold), *he's gone to Heaven, no doubt—but he won't like God.*

—Robert Louis Stevenson

I knew Doris Day before she became a virgin.

—Oscar Levant

Jackie Robinson couldn't hit an inside pitch to save his neck.

—Bob Feller

Told that Clare Boothe Luce was unfailingly kind to her inferiors, Dorothy Parker asked, ''Where does she find them?''

Italian journalist Oriana Fallaci's description of Henry Kissinger: *an eel icier than ice.*

> *George the Third*
> *Ought never to have occurred.*
> *One can only wonder*
> *At so grotesque a blunder.*
>
> —E. Clerihew Bentley

It was very good of God to let Carlyle and Mrs. Carlyle marry one another and so make only two people miserable instead of four.

—Samuel Butler

If I were a rich man, I would employ a professional praiser.

—Sir Osbert Sitwell

Oops! Sorry About That!

I can pardon everyone's mistakes but my own.

—Cato

An American businessman, in New Zealand during the visit of Queen Elizabeth II, found himself suddenly face-to-face with Her Majesty. He curtsied.

Workmen in Cincinnati who were building a fire escape on the Wanda Lee apartments accidentally set the building on fire.

William Henry Harrison delivered his two-hour inaugural address on a blustery March day wearing no overcoat, hat, or gloves. He caught a cold, which turned into pneumonia. One month later he was dead.

Virginia Woolf's vague sister, Vanessa, casting about for something to say to her dinner partner, Mr. Herbert Asquith, asked if he were interested in politics. The mild-mannered gentleman admitted that he was. He happened to be the prime minister of England.

Dorothy Parker died in a shabby hotel room in impoverished circumstances. Police later found in a drawer a ten thousand dollar check which she had mislaid.

> *Theirs not to reason why;*
> *Theirs but to do and die;*
> *Into the valley of Death*
> *Rode the six hundred . . .*
>
> —Alfred Lord Tennyson

In the Crimean War, a command was given for the British Light Brigade to charge into a valley heavily fortified by enemy Russian artillery. The irrational order was passed down the line by the stiff-lipped officers of the British high command, none of whom wanted his peers to think he lacked courage. Within twenty minutes, nearly half the troops had been killed or wounded.

Dick Stuart, first baseman for the Boston Red Sox, Pittsburgh Pirates, and Philadelphia Phillies, seven times led the major leagues in errors. A Boston sportswriter called him ''Dr. Strangeglove.''

In 1915 *The Washington Post* reported that President Wilson had escorted his fiancée, Edith Galt, to the theater. The story related that the president had paid less attention to the play than to entertaining Mrs. Galt. A misprint stated that he was busy all evening "entering" Mrs. Galt.

The Metropolitan Museum's famous bronze cat, revered for twenty-five years as an ancient Egyptian artifact, was revealed in the spring of 1987 to be "in all probability" a modern forgery.

Elvis Presley was turned down in 1955 by *Arthur Godfrey's Talent Scouts*.

Diamond Jim Brady, believing he was about to die, burned twenty thousand dollars in promissory notes owed to him by his friends. Then he got well.

Columbia Pictures let Marilyn Monroe's contract lapse in 1949 because producer Harry Cohn felt she lacked "star quality."

Adam Smith, pseudonymous author of *The Money Game* and *Super Money*, let himself get talked out of buying Tampax stock at $5 a share. "I feel dumb every time I think about it," he confessed a few years later when Tampax was selling at $120.

Faced with his first artichoke at a black tie dinner, theologian Reinhold Niebuhr failed to notice that his fellow guests were delicately dipping their leaves into the sauce. He poured his hollandaise over the entire artichoke.

It is very easy to forgive others their mistakes. It takes more gut and gumption to forgive them for having witnessed your own.

—Jessamyn West

It is understandable that George Sand's letter to her former lover, Alfred de Musset, failed to win him back:

I go nearly mad, I soak my pillow with tears, I hear in the silence of the night your voice calling me . . . Good-bye my dearest little one . . . Good-bye, Alfred, love your George. Send me, I beg, twelve pairs of glacé gloves, six yellow and six of color.

At the funeral of French president, Georges Pompidou, President Nixon declared, "This is a great day for France."

That is not what I meant at all. That is not it at all.

—T. S. Eliot

Thomas J. Watson, chairman of the board of IBM, said in 1943, ''I think there is a world market for about five computers.''

Christopher Columbus went to his death believing that the islands he discovered were just west of Japan.

In 1964 Jim Marshall of the Minnesota Vikings scooped up a football from the rival team's fumble and ran with it sixty yards in the wrong direction into his own team's end zone, thereby scoring two points for the opposing San Francisco Forty-Niners.

The London *Guardian* ran a review of the opera *Doris Gudenov*.

The *Queen Elizabeth II*'s maiden voyage from Southampton to New York after a $130 million overhaul was plagued by blanketless beds, broken air-conditioning, empty swimming pools, non-working plumbing, flooded cabins, and labor problems. Sheepish Cunard officials offered irate passengers a forty per cent rebate.

Over seventy-five million pieces of mail end up each year in the dead letter office.

A 1631 edition of the Bible omitted one word. The Seventh Commandment read, ''Thou shalt commit adultery.''

On an August night in 1977, David Berkowitz parked his car too close to a fire hydrant in Brooklyn. The thirty-five-dollar ticket slapped on the car led police to evidence that Berkowitz was the Son of Sam who had terrorized New York in a year-long series of nighttime attacks.

On a visit to Kuala Lumpur, Mrs. Reagan was invited to tea with the Queen of Malaysia at the royal palace. The First Lady's entourage was cautioned not to wear yellow or blue, the royal colors, or white, because it is a funeral color. On the appointed hour, Mrs. Reagan showed up in a white dress with blue flowers, blue shoes, and a blue straw hat.

Robbers worked diligently to dig a tunnel to the vault floor of the Hamilton, Washington State Bank, which had been out of business for four years.

According to Sigmund Freud, there was a right and a wrong kind of female orgasm. The good one was the grown-up, truly fulfilling vaginal type; bad was the trivial, childish clitoral variety. It took science several decades to discover that Dr. Freud's theory should long since have been tossed out with antimacassars and other useless relics of the Victorian era.

Columbia Pictures and Metro-Goldwyn-Mayer had no interest in putting money into *Away We Go*, a down-on-the-farm stage musical with no stars and no chorus line. Other investors concurred that it lacked pizzazz and had no future. Financing was scraped up in bits and pieces, and the show opened in New Haven to mixed reactions. The second act was rewritten, a new production number added, and a decision made to change the name of the show. It opened on Broadway as *Oklahoma!*

Alexander Graham Bell offered Western Union exclusive rights to his "talking machine" for $100,000. Western Union president William Orton turned down the offer with a rhetorical question: "What use could this company make of an electrical toy?"

Henri Matisse's painting, *Le Bateau*, hung forty-seven days in the Museum of Modern Art before someone noticed it was upside down.

> *"I didn't know you could lay eggs," said Wilbur in amazement.*
> *"Oh, sure," said the spider. "I'm versatile."*
> *"What does 'versatile' mean—full of eggs?" asked Wilbur.*

> Charlotte's Web
> —E. B. White

Mithridates VI, king of Pontus in the first-century B.C., regularly swallowed toxic substances to make himself immune to murder by poison. When Mithridates faced defeat by Pompey and tried to kill himself by swallowing poison, it had no effect. He commanded a slave to run a sword through him.

Two Chicago thieves were caught because they failed to take with them a camera when they robbed a house. The owner had the film developed. It contained a snapshot one burglar had taken of the other.

When Dante Gabriel Rossetti's wife died, he placed in her tomb the poems he had written to her. It was a touching and penitent gesture toward the woman to whom he had been consistently unfaithful. It also turned out to be a not-very-good idea. Before long, Rossetti became convinced that the buried poems were the best work he'd done, but he couldn't recall how they went. After brooding for seven years, Rossetti had the grave dug up. The rescued poems were published to considerable acclaim.

Irving Thalberg persuaded Louis B. Mayer not to film *Gone with the Wind* because "no Civil War picture has ever made a nickel."

The letter notifying Zachary Taylor that he had been nominated for the presidency was sent postage-due by the Whig Committee. Taylor refused to pay the ten cents, and the letter languished for weeks in the dead letter office.

An 1895 plot to overthrow the Manchu regime in China called for an army of mercenaries to assemble in Hong Kong and board ferry boats to Canton as ordinary passengers. Along with them would go barrels labeled "Portland Cement" that were actually filled with ammunition. While waiting on the dock, the mercenaries began fighting over who would get the best guns. They missed the boat, and the coup missed its chance to happen.

Ronald Reagan was rejected for the leading role in the 1964 movie *The Best Man* because "he doesn't look like a president."

Less than a week after Lee Iacocca was named by Körbel Champagne one of the Top Ten Romantic People of 1986, he filed for divorce from his wife, Peggy.

Captain Robert Scott, leader of the British expedition to the South Pole, made a calamitous decision to use ponies instead of dogs to pull the sleds. Chosen for their superior strength, the heavy ponies sank up to their bellies in the soft, fresh snow. Eventually all had to be mercifully shot, and the men pulled their own supplies. Most probably the Scott expedition had no chance of reaching the Pole before the well-equipped Norwegian expedition under Amundsen, but the use of dogs could have saved the lives of Scott and the four men who died on the terrible return journey.

Mark Twain used the large royalties he made from his books to invest in high-risk business ventures. His get-poor-quick schemes included a hemorrhoid cure, a public bath, a silver mine, and self-adjusting suspenders that didn't work.

Singer Little Richard was offered a fifty percent interest in the Beatles by their manager, Brian Epstein. He turned it down because he couldn't see any future for the group.

Warren Austin, U.S. ambassador to the United Nations in 1948, expressed the wish that Arabs and Jews would settle their differences "like good Christians."

If President Lincoln were alive today, he'd roll over in his grave.

—President Gerald Ford

At an elegant dinner given at Delmonico's restaurant in 1873, the centerpiece was a thirty-foot oval pond in which floated four heavily sedated swans. As the evening went on, the drugs wore off, and the swans underwent a personality change from serene to pugnacious. They stalked from the pond, dripping, flapping, and pecking viciously at one another, to assert their right to brandy and bonbons.

According to a survey, American businesses waste $2.6 million annually on unnecessary photocopies. Of the 350 billion photocopies made each year, an estimated 130 billion are thrown into the wastepaper basket.

In 1908, the New York Giants lost the pennant to the Chicago Cubs because player Fred Merkle missed second when he rounded the bases.

A young woman in Hermosa Beach, California, left her two children outside a bank while she went in, brandished a threatening note, and left with four thousand dollars. Several persons saw her collect her children and vanish. A short time later she was discovered sitting with her little ones in the next-door escrow department of the same bank, waiting for the taxi she'd asked a teller to order for her.

Alexander Woollcott left orders for his ashes to be buried on the campus of Hamilton College, his alma mater. The ashes, mailed by his friends, arrived at Hamilton with sixty-seven cents postage due.

An error in the Sunday business section incorrectly said Brooke Astor and Mrs. Walter Annenberg are socialists. The word should have read socialites.

The Cincinnati Enquirer

In 1853 John Coffee built the jail in Dundalk, Ireland. He went bankrupt on the project and became the first inmate of his own jail.

When William Howard Taft was in the White House, he continually referred to his predecessor, Theodore Roosevelt, as "the president."

I once undertook on behalf of a friend to smuggle a small dog through the customs. I was of ample propor-

tions, and managed to conceal the little dog upon my person. All went well until my bosom barked.

—Mrs. Patrick Campbell, British actress

On Queen Elizabeth's 1984 visit to the United States, she and President Reagan took to the floor to open the dancing. At that precise moment, the band struck up a sprightly rendition of "The Lady is a Tramp."

Advertisements once touted L&M cigarettes as "just what the doctor ordered."

Had architect Bonanno chosen a construction site with firm subsoil, the bell tower he built in Pisa in the twelfth century would have stood up straight as a tower properly should; in which event, the town of Pisa, eight centuries later, would not be filled with tourists snapping photos of one another standing in front of a bell tower that leans fourteen feet out of perpendicular; and souvenir hawkers and gelato vendors in present-day Pisa would lack for enough customers to make a decent living.

So. Every now and then a mistake turns out for the best.

Other Times and Places

A brisk trot through bygone times won't cure the strains and stresses often referred to as what-we-put-up-with-nowadays. It may, however, prove that you and I didn't pick the worst time in the history of the world to be alive.

History never looks like history when you are living through it. It always looks confusing and messy, and it always feels uncomfortable.

—John W. Gardner

Tour d'Argent, Paris' oldest restaurant, served dormouse pastries when it opened in 1533.

Emperor Justinian permitted divorce by mutual consent on the condition that both husband and wife vow to abstain from sex during the remainder of their lives.

The world had to struggle along without safety pins until 1849.

The *A* for adultery that Hester Prynne wore in *The Scarlet Letter* was only one of several letters that lawbreakers were forced to wear as punishment during the seventeenth and eighteenth centuries in the Massachusetts Bay Colony. Others were *B* for blasphemy, *F* for forgery, *D* for drunkenness, *R* for rape, *P* for poisoning, *T* for theft and *V* for viciousness.

In nineteenth century England it became fashionable for women to wear gold rings in their nipples.

When the sugarcoated wedding cake first appeared in England during the reign of Charles II, it was traditionally broken over the head of the bride and the fragments distributed to the guests. Eventually it occurred to someone that the cake might more nicely be served with a knife.

Shoes were worn interchangeably on either foot until 1800, when King George IV ordered boots made specifically to fit his right and left feet.

In 1659 Massachusetts passed a law banning Christmas. Fines were levied on scofflaws who sang carols or put up sprigs of mistletoe.

At the turn of the century it was unacceptable in polite society to speak of a chicken breast or leg. The refined terms were "white meat" and "first joint."

Cleopatra was the product of six generations of brother-sister marriages.

In 1789 life expectancy for Americans was 36.5 years for females and 34.5 years for males—a marked improvement over Neanderthal times, when less than half the population survived to the age of twenty.

In colonial days, a book was viewed as harmful if it stimulated a child's imagination or provided amusement.

Because of the heavy traffic in Rome, Julius Caesar banned all wheeled vehicles during the daytime hours.

The Sears-Roebuck catalog of 1909 carried an advertisement for a horseless buggy that was "guaranteed to go one hundred miles in twenty-four hours if good care is taken of it."

Ancient Egyptians shaved off all their body hair.

Dr. John B. Watson, in his 1928 book, *The Psychological Care of Infant and Child*, warned parents not to spoil their children with unnecessary displays of affection: *Never hug and kiss them, never let them sit in your lap.* Psychologist Watson recommended that parents shake hands with their children each morning.

Louis XIV, the most elegant man in seventeenth-century Europe, took a bath once a year.

Twenty-one people drowned in molasses when a storage tank ruptured in Boston harbor in 1919. Eight buildings on Commercial Street were engulfed in a wave of syrup fifty feet high.

The world is a very dangerous place. It's no wonder nobody ever gets out of it alive.

—Graffito

In ancient Japan, public contests were held to determine who in town could fart loudest and longest.

In *The Young Wife* (1837), William A. Alcott noted with alarm that not only men but women used "coarse, vulgar words" . . . such as "*My Stars!*" "*My Soul!*" "*By George!*" and "*Good Heavens!*" Alcott proclaimed that "such words, besides being indelicate, savor not a little of profanity."

In France in the time of Louis XI, public executions were celebrated as fêtes.

In 1633, Sultan Murad IV of Turkey ordered tobacco users hanged, beheaded, or starved to death.

The average American woman in the seventeenth century gave birth to thirteen children.

A Timetable For Boiling Vegetables

Young beets, young turnips, young carrots, parsnips, sweet and Irish potatoes, string beans   45 minutes

New onions, new cabbage, winter squash, oyster plants, cauliflower, shelled beans, shelled peas   1 hour

Winter carrots, onions, cabbage, turnips, beets, mushrooms   2 hours

—Aunt Babette's Cook Book (1889)

In 1658 the Virginia legislature passed a law expelling all lawyers from the colony. They weren't allowed back until 1680.

People who couldn't pay their debts in ancient Rome had a choice of being cut up with a dull ax or pulled apart by wild horses.

A transvestite was governor of New York for six years. Lord Cornbury, appointed by Queen Anne in 1702, appeared at ceremonial occasions wearing a dress, silk stockings, high heels, and an elaborate wig. Finally, incensed New Yorkers forced his recall.

During the siege of Paris in 1871, animals in the Paris zoo were slaughtered for food. One pound of elephant trunk cost forty francs.

In 1845, the average female mill worker in Massachusetts earned $1.75 a week, and worked from 5 A.M. to 7 P.M. with a half hour for lunch. In 1847, the lunch period was extended by twenty minutes. Six years later, the work day was reduced to eleven hours.

During the reign of Edward III it was illegal for wives of men under the rank of knight to wear jewellery.

In 1656 Captain Kemble of Boston was sentenced to two hours in the public stocks for "lewd and unseemly behavior in kissing his wife publiquely on the Sabbath." The depraved deed took place on Captain Kemble's own doorstep upon his return from a three-year sea voyage.

In Czarist Russia, brides presented their husbands-to-be with whips they had made themselves as symbols of submission.

A current edition of *The New York Times* contains more information than could be picked up in an entire lifetime before the sixteenth century.

In 1685, when Charles II became ill, physicians (1) drew a pint of blood from his veins; (2) poured antimony and sulfate of zinc down his throat to make him vomit; (3) gave him an enema; (4) shaved his head and singed his scalp with red hot irons; (5) dabbed his face and feet with pigeon droppings; (6) covered him with hot plasters; (7) fed him pearls dissolved in ammonia, and powder from a human skull; (8) administered sixteen more enemas; (9) filled his nose with sneezing powder; (10) dosed him with purgatives, laxatives, sedatives, heart tonics, and antidotes for poison; (11) gave him another enema; (12) drew another twelve ounces of blood. On the fifth day, King Charles mercifully, and probably thankfully, died.

In 1929, only eight percent of American families had incomes over five thousand dollars. Sixty percent lived on less than two thousand dollars a year, which, even in those days, wouldn't buy the basic necessities of life.

In early-seventeenth-century France, cavaliers streaked their hair and dabbed rouge on their cheeks.

In ancient Egypt only pharaohs were allowed to eat mushrooms. They were considered too good for anyone else.

In England in the eighteenth-century (a.k.a. the Age of Enlightenment) death by hanging was the punishment for 223 crimes, including theft of one shilling's worth of goods.

STRAIGHT FRONT FINE BATISTE CORSET, Bias Gored, . . . military erect figure . . . 2 side steels and 4 bone strips with extra heavy front, 10-inch steel bound underneath . . . medium weight with a low bust . . . Handsomely trimmed . . . pretty lace . . .

—Sears-Roebuck Catalog, 1905

Life is not a spectacle or a feast. It is a predicament.

—George Santayana

Early Crusaders sometimes cooked and ate their victims. One chronicler claimed they tasted better than spiced peacock.

Until 1870 people had to manage without paper clips.

In the Middle Ages barely one person in twenty could read and write.

In Victorian times blushing ladies considered piano legs so embarrassingly like human limbs that they covered them with skirts.

April, 1955

Dear Bill:
Life in New York continues jolly, but it would be much jollier if crime was not so rife. It's all the go here these days. The liquor store a few blocks from where we are was looted a few days ago, and last week Ethel was held up at a dressmaker's on Madison Avenue. She was in the middle of being fitted when a man came in brandishing a knife and asked for contributions. He got eighteen dollars from her and disappeared into the void . . .

—*P. G. Wodehouse*

Until 1913 the world existed without crossword puzzles.

. . . the full force of sexual desire is seldom known to a virtuous woman.

—Dr. William Sanger (1859)

In France during the Age of Chivalry, unmarried women could own only one dress unless they were heiresses who had inherited castles.

Essentials for the Laundry

Clothes boiler, copper bottomed
Washboard
Ironing board
2 Tubs
Flatirons
Iron rest
Clothes bars
Clothes basket
Clothesline & clothespins

—*The Ladies' Home Journal,* 1905

In 1619, potatoes were banned in Burgundy because eating too many of them was thought to cause leprosy. In Switzerland potatoes were blamed for scrofula.

In Germany in the seventeenth century, King Frederick William decided potatoes could solve a food shortage and ordered peasants who refused to plant them to have their noses and ears cut off.

Drug abuse was a major problem in the United States in the late 1800s, when addictive substances were used in many pharmaceutical products. Cocaine tablets were prescribed for throat and nerves, baby syrups were spiked with morphine, and heroin was marketed as cough medicine.

The perfect hostess will see to it that the works of male and female authors be properly separated on her book-

shelves. Their proximity, unless they happen to be married, should not be tolerated.

—Lady Gough's Etiquette (1863)

In the 1830s making a daguerreotype required subjects to sit in full sunlight without moving a muscle for nearly twenty minutes. To ensure absolute stillness, their heads were fastened into clamps.

Nostalgia is a seductive liar.

—George W. Ball

Assorted Solaces

A blessing to count on a day when you can't think of any.

It's your good fortune not to live in the Karachev-Cherkessk autonomous region in southwestern Russia. Its ninety thousand or so inhabitants use the Abyssinian alphabet, which has 73 letters. How'd you like to be a file clerk in Cherkessk? Look up a telephone number? Use a dictionary? Teach that 73-letter alphabet to your kids?

A cause for rejoicing when you're working on your income tax

Roman numerals, in general use throughout the world for nearly two thousand years, were superseded by Arabic numbers. Had that not happened, you'd have to

119

compute VII.XV percent of your, say, $XLVMDCCVI salary to figure your Social Security tax.

Five points to consider when you're feeling sorry for yourself

1. If you were a squirrel, you'd see only in black and white.
2. If you were a butterfly, you'd have your taste buds on the soles of your feet.
3. If you were a snake, you'd never dream.
4. If you were a cat, you couldn't taste anything sweet.
5. If you were an Atlantic keeled snail, you'd spend your whole life swimming upside down.

A quick fix for a negative self-image

If you wince at your reflection in the bathroom mirror as you emerge naked and dripping from the shower, you'd do well to sign up for a swim class. Not because the exercise will firm your muscle tone (albeit that's a possibility) but because you'll pick up some valuable insights in the locker-room showers. One quick look around should convince you that nobody in real life looks like a *Penthouse* centerfold or Michelangelo's *David*.

A miracle to thank your lucky stars for

Your opposable thumbs. Only primates have them, and they are a transcendent gift. If you can't see why they're so wonderful, tuck your thumbs into your palms. Now try to tie your shoe, throw a ball, light a match, write your name. See? Without those phenomenal thumbs, civilization wouldn't have progressed to the Stone Age.

Five reasons you're lucky not to be a man.

1. Men are six times more likely than women to be struck by lightning.
2. Mosquitoes bite men more often than women.
3. Women don't get hiccups as frequently as men.
4. Research shows that women give clearer and better walking directions than men do.
5. The average woman's driving reaction time is ten times faster than the average man's.

Five reasons you're lucky not to be a woman.

1. Men are less likely than women to be knock-kneed.
2. Males are better than females at finding their way out of a maze.
3. Men are ten times more likely than women to make more than fifty thousand dollars a year.
4. It is unusual for a man to be kept awake by a snoring spouse.
5. Men are speedier than women at making up their minds what to order from a menu.

An exclusive privilege

Only you (that is, only you and the five billion or so other human beings on this planet) can make love all year round. Anytime-sex is an indulgence enjoyed only by homo sapiens. For all other living creatures, sex goes in and out of season, like fresh peaches and college football.

A point to ponder when life seems dull and uneventful

If you think *your* existence is humdrum, consider those poor souls in TV commercials who get all excited about a fresher-smelling fabric softener, and for whom it's a peak experience to discover some raisins in their breakfast cereal.

A consolation after you've made a fool of yourself

You're probably not a member of a major league ball team. *Your* errors, unless they are truly spectacular, don't show up in the morning paper.

A blessing to be grateful for on Thanksgiving

At Bedouin feasts, the pièce de résistance is roast camel stuffed with a whole sheep.

Two major reasons not to bewail your luck

1) Sixty to eighty percent of the world's population has never tasted chocolate.
2) The average number of spermatozoa discharged in a single human ejaculation is estimated at 135,000,000. When you consider the odds against

the one that outraced the others to fertilize the egg that turned into the embryo that became *you* you've got to feel lucky to be here.

About the Author

JANE GOODSELL is a lifelong resident of Portland, Oregon, a circumstance which, she says, ''shows both an unadventurous spirit and good judgment.'' Her other works include *I've Only Got Two Hands and I'm Busy Wringing Them* and several books for children, including *Toby's Toe*. Her biography of Daniel Inouye won the Carter G. Woodson Award in 1978.